KRYPTOON

life lessons by minions

life be banana

Copyright © 2024 by kryptoon

This is a fan-made parody book inspired by the Minions characters. Minions and all related characters are trademarks and copyrights of Universal Studios and Illumination Entertainment. This book is not authorized, sponsored, or endorsed by Universal Studios, Illumination Entertainment, or any entities associated with the Despicable Me franchise. All original content in this work is © 2024 by Kryptoon and may not be reproduced without permission. This is a work of parody and is intended for entertainment purposes only. A portion of proceeds will be donated to mental health charities. Remember, imitation is the sincerest form of banana-ry!

First edition

This book was professionally typeset on Reedsy. Find out more at reedsy.com

Introduction

Bello, bello, banana-lovers and giggly-wiggly friends! Get ready for a wild ride of laughter, wisdom, and pure Minionese madness! In this book-book, we've gathered 300 bananatastic life lessons, straight from the yellow minds of your favorite minion amigos.

From "Gelato brain freeze olympics" to "Life speak whale to goldfish," these quoty-woties are packed with silly-willy humor and smarty-pants advice. Whether you're feeling poopaye in the dumpy-wumpies or up in cloudy-wowdies, these banana-bonkers wisdom chunks will make you scratch your heady-weddy, go hahaha in belly, and maybe even go loco-coco in thinky-brain (but good way)!

So grab your yummiest yellow fruit, put on your googly-woogly glasses, and get ready to jumpy-bumpy into a world where underwear can be superhero masky-wasky and life's uh-oh-spaghetti-os about no more bananas!

BANANA

"No like banana? Peel-ieve in yourself!"

BANANA

"When life give lemons, make banana smoothie!"

BANANA

"Trouble sleep? Count bananas, not boring sheep!"

BANANA

"Want be happy? Wear underpants on head!"

BANANA

"Feel blue? Paint yourself yellow!"

BANANA

"Bad hair day? Stick banana on top, instant mohawk!"

BANANA

"Can't dance? Pretend floor is lava, instant moves!"

BANANA

"Tired of working? Become banana!"

BANANA

"Want friends? Learn fart language!"

A

"Feeling short? Stand on tall banana pile!"

BANANA

"Bad breath? Eat more bananas, poop less onions!"

BANANA

"Want be strong? Lift bananas, not boring weights!"

BANANA

"Scared of dark? Glow-in-dark underpants solve everything!"

BANANA

"No money? Print banana currency!"

BANANA

"Lonely? Hug cactus, make prickly friend!"

BANANA

"Want be smart? Wear banana peel as thinking cap!"

BANANA

"Bored? Start fire with banana friction!"

BANANA

"Can't sing? Yodel in helium voice!"

BANANA

"Want be famous? Invent banana-flavored air!"

AA

"Feeling lazy? Roll downhill like happy banana!"

BANANA

"Bad at cooking? Banana goes with everything!"

BANANA

"Want be fashionable? Wear banana as bowtie!"

BANANA

"Can't focus? Stick googly eyes on forehead!"

BANANA

"Forget something? Tie banana to memory!"

BANANA

"Want be cool? Wear sunglasses on butt!"

BANANA

"Feel ugly? Put banana peel on face, instant beauty mask!"

BANANA

"Can't make decision? Ask Magic Banana 8-Ball!"

BANANA

"Want be fit? Chase ice cream truck every day!"

BANANA

"Bad at math? Count in bananas!"

AAA

"Feel stressed? Scream into banana like phone!"

BANANA

"Want be romantic? Serenade with banana guitar!"

BANANA

"Can't write? Use banana as pen!"

BANANA

"Feel weak? Eat spinach, become Popeye-minion!"

BANANA

"Want be rich? Start banana black market!"

BANANA

"Bad at sports? Invent banana-ball, be champion!"

BANANA

"Can't stop procrastinating? Set clock to banana time!"

BANANA

"Feel cold? Wear banana peel as scarf!"

BANANA

"Want be popular? Learn banana juggling!"

BANANA

"Bad at public speaking? Imagine audience as bananas!"

AAAA

"Can't wake up? Alarm clock that shoots bananas!"

BANANA

"Feel short-tempered? Count to banana before reacting!"

BANANA

"Want be adventurous? Banana-peel surfing!"

BANANA

"Bad at saving money? Use banana-shaped piggy bank!"

BANANA

"Can't remember names? Call everyone 'Banana'!"

BANANA

"Feel unappreciated? Give self 'Best Minion' award!"

BANANA

"Want be artist? Paint with banana mush!"

BANANA

"Bad at directions? Follow banana peel trail!"

BANANA

"Can't stop eating? Banana-only diet!"

BANANA

"Feel uninspired? Wear banana costume to work!"

AAAAA

"Want be leader? Crown self Banana King/Queen!"

BANANA

"Can't swim? Use banana as floatie!"

BANANA

"Want be ninja? Practice sneaking with squeaky banana shoes!"

BANANA

"Bad at gardening? Plant banana trees everywhere!"

BANANA

"Feel powerless? Wear banana peel as superhero cape!"

BANANA

"Can't stop hiccups? Eat banana upside-down!"

BANANA

"Want be magician? Make bananas disappear in mouth!"

BANANA

"Bad at yoga? Do 'peeling banana' pose!"

BANANA

"Feel invisible? Wear banana suit, be center of attention!"

BANANA

"Can't sleep? Count sheep riding bananas!"

AAAAAA

"Want be weather reporter? Forecast banana storms!"

BANANA

"Bad at cleaning? Use banana peel as mop!"

BANANA

"Feel sad? Tickle self with banana leaf!"

BANANA

"Can't make friends? Offer free banana hugs!"

BANANA

"Want be astronaut? Build rocket from banana peels!"

BANANA

"Bad at sports? Become professional banana peeler!"

BANANA

"Feel boring? Wear underwear outside pants!"

BANANA

"Can't stop laughing? Think about serious bananas!"

BANANA

"Want be detective? Follow trail of banana peels!"

BANANA

"Bad breath? Brush teeth with banana toothpaste!"

AAAAAAA

"Feel unlucky? Carry lucky banana charm!"

BANANA

"Can't write novel? Tell banana knock-knock jokes instead!"

BANANA

"Want be musician? Join banana percussion band!"

BANANA

"Bad at math? Calculate everything in banana units!"

BANANA

"Feel stressed? Do banana breathing exercises!"

BANANA

"Can't dance? Move like jelly in earthquake!"

BANANA

"Want be fashion designer? Make clothes from banana leaves!"

BANANA

"Bad at drawing? Trace banana shadows!"

BANANA

"Feel tired? Take power nap in banana hammock!"

BANANA

"Can't make decisions? Flip a banana instead of coin!"

AAAAAAA

"Want be strong? Lift giant inflatable bananas!"

BANANA

"Bad at singing? Yodel in banana language!"

BANANA

"Feel clumsy? Wear banana peel shoes for grip!"

BANANA

"Can't focus? Wear horse blinders made of banana leaves!"

BANANA

"Want be popular? Start banana-themed social media!"

BANANA

"Bad at cooking? Everything tastes better banana-battered!"

BANANA

"Feel short? Wear banana peel platform shoes!"

BANANA

"Can't grow mustache? Stick banana peel on upper lip!"

BANANA

"Want be organized? Use banana-shaped sticky notes!"

BANANA

"Bad at parallel parking? Use bananas as bumpers!"

AAAAAAAA

"Feel nervous? Squeeze stress-relief banana!"

BANANA

"Can't remember anniversaries? Mark calendar with banana stickers!"

BANANA

"Want be explorer? Map uncharted banana territories!"

BANANA

"Bad at poetry? Write banana haikus!"

BANANA

"Feel cold? Knit sweater from banana peels!"

BANANA

"Can't wake up? Set alarm to 'banana phone' ring tone!"

BANANA

"Want be successful? Climb corporate banana tree!"

BANANA

"Bad at sports? Become professional banana boat racer!"

BANANA

"Feel pessimistic? Always look at banana's yellow side!"

BANANA

"Can't stop procrastinating? Reward self with banana for each task!"

AAAAAAAAA

"Want be movie star? Star in 'Attack of the Killer Bananas'!"

BANANA

"Bad at public speaking? Imagine audience as bunch of bananas!"

BANANA

"Feel uninspired? Wear banana peel as thinking cap!"

BANANA

"Want be mime? Practice 'trapped in banana peel' routine!"

BANANA

"Bad at gambling? Play banana slot machines!"

BANANA

"Feel too serious? Wear banana peel eyebrows!"

BANANA

"Can't ride bike? Use banana seat for extra cushion!"

BANANA

"Want be ventriloquist? Use banana as dummy!"

BANANA

"Bad at DIY? Build furniture with banana crates!"

BANANA

"Feel too tall? Measure self in mini-bananas!"

AAAAAAAAAA

"Can't stop gossip? Tell secrets to banana bunch!"

BANANA

"Want be olympian? Compete in banana luge!"

BANANA

"Bad at gardening? Grow banana bonsai trees!"

BANANA

"Feel too clean? Take mud bath with banana chunks!"

BANANA

"Can't stop laughing? Think about serious bananas in suits!"

BANANA

"Want be ninja? Practice banana-peel stealth walking!"

BANANA

"Bad at chess? Use banana pieces, king is whole bunch!"

BANANA

"Feel too quiet? Become banana-themed carnival barker!"

BANANA

"Can't ice skate? Wear banana peel skates!"

BANANA

"Want be sommelier? Become expert in banana wine tasting!"

AAAAAAAAAA

"Bad at knitting? Use banana fibers as yarn!"

BANANA

"Feel too organized? Sort everything by banana shape!"

BANANA

"Can't blow bubbles? Use banana-flavored soap!"

BANANA

"Want be paleontologist? Dig for fossilized bananas!"

BANANA

"Bad at bowling? Use banana as pin, coconut as ball!"

BANANA

"Feel too flexible? Do banana-peel resistance training!"

BANANA

"Can't play golf? Use banana as club, grape as ball!"

BANANA

"Want be fortune teller? Read banana peel patterns!"

BANANA

"Bad at juggling? Start with soft, squishy bananas!"

BANANA

"Feel too grumpy? Stick banana smile on face!"

AAAAAAAAAAA

"Can't play drums? Use banana bunches as bongos!"

BANANA

"Want be conductor? Lead banana peel orchestra!"

BANANA

"Bad at origami? Fold banana peels into animals!"

BANANA

"Feel too heavy? Weigh self on banana scale!"

BANANA

"Can't stop nail-biting? Wear banana peel finger guards!"

BANANA

"Want be filmmaker? Direct 'Attack of Killer Bananas' movie!"

BANANA

"Bad at card tricks? Use deck made of banana-shaped cards!"

BANANA

"Feel too predictable? Wear banana peel backwards!"

BANANA

"Can't hula hoop? Use giant banana peel as hoop!"

BANANA

"Want be radio host? Start 'All Banana, All The Time' station!"

AAAAAAAAAAAA

"Bad at charades? Act out 'Life of Banana' every time!"

BANANA

"Feel too inflexible? Do banana-peel yoga!"

BANANA

"Can't play tennis? Use banana as racket, grape as ball!"

BANANA

"Want be botanist? Classify 1001 types of bananas!"

BANANA

"Bad at hide-and-seek? Hide in pile of banana peels!"

BANANA

"Feel too mature? Have banana costume party for no reason!"

BANANA

"Can't stop sweating? Use banana peel antiperspirant!"

BANANA

"Want be zoologist? Study banana slug behavior!"

BANANA

"Bad at surfing? Ride giant banana peel surfboard!"

BANANA

"Feel too carnivorous? Become banana-tarian!"

AAAAAAAAAAAAAA

"Can't play soccer? Use coconut as ball, banana as goal post!"

BANANA

"Want be tattoo artist? Specialize in banana ink designs!"

BANANA

"Bad at rock climbing? Scale wall of banana crates!"

BANANA

"Feel too terrestrial? Build banana rocket to moon!"

BANANA

"Can't do magic? Pull banana out of ear trick never fail!"

BANANA

"Want be food critic? Become expert in banana ripeness!"

BANANA

"Bad at crosswords? All answers are banana-related!"

BANANA

"Feel too awake? Count banana sheep jumping fence!"

BANANA

"Can't whistle? Use banana peel as whistle!"

BANANA

"Want be archaeologist? Dig for ancient banana civilizations!"

AAAAAAAAAAAAAAA

"Bad at sudoku? Fill squares with banana stickers!"

BANANA

"Feel too dry? Use banana peel as humidifier!"

BANANA

"Can't draw straight line? Use banana as ruler!"

BANANA

"Want be therapist? Counsel people using banana puppets!"

BANANA

"Bad at darts? Throw banana peels at banana-shaped board!"

BANANA

"Feel too colorful? See world through banana-tinted glasses!"

BANANA

"Can't stop sneezing? Wear banana peel nose guard!"

BANANA

"Want be taxidermist? Stuff giant bananas instead of animals!"

BANANA

"Bad at parkour? Practice jumping over banana obstacles!"

BANANA

"Feel too noisy? Use banana as sound-dampening headphones!"

AAAAAAAAAAAAAAAA

"Can't play guitar? Make one from hollow banana bunch!"

BANANA

"Want be journalist? Write for 'The Daily Banana' newspaper!"

BANANA

"Bad at makeup? Use mashed banana as face paint!"

BANANA

"Feel too landlocked? Build banana-shaped submarine!"

BANANA

"Can't play basketball? Use peeled banana as hoop!"

BANANA

"Want be voice actor? Specialize in banana commercial voices!"

BANANA

"Bad at finger painting? Use banana pudding instead!"

BANANA

"Feel too vertical? Practice banana-peel limbo!"

BANANA

"Can't ride horse? Saddle up giant banana instead!"

BANANA

"Want be perfumer? Create eau de banana fragrance!"

AAAAAAAAAAAAAAAAA

"Bad at table tennis? Use banana half as paddle!"

BANANA

"Feel too earthbound? Fly banana-copter to work!"

BANANA

"Can't solve crimes? Join banana peel forensics team!"

BANANA

"Want be competitive eater? Specialize in banana speed peeling!"

BANANA

"Bad at pilates? Do banana-resistance exercises!"

BANANA

"Feel too rigid? Practice 'banana in the wind' dance moves!"

BANANA

"Can't play piano? Try banana-key keyboard instead!"

BANANA

"Want be paranormal investigator? Hunt for banana ghosts!"

BANANA

"Bad at roller skating? Wear banana peel roller skates!"

BANANA

"Feel too talkative? Use banana as 'quiet stick' in meetings!"

AAAAAAAAAAAAAAAAAAAA

"Can't trim hedges? Shape shrubs into banana designs!"

BANANA

"Want be virtual assistant? Change name to Banana-Alexa!"

BANANA

"Bad at hopscotch? Draw course with banana pudding!"

BANANA

"Feel too terrestrial? Imagine life as banana on Mars!"

BANANA

"Can't sleep in dark? Use banana-shaped night light!"

BANANA

"Want be professional mourner? Attend funerals of old bananas!"

BANANA

"Bad at ping pong? Use banana as paddle, grape as ball!"

BANANA

"Feel too logical? Make decisions based on banana oracle!"

BANANA

"Can't bake bread? Make banana-only sourdough starter!"

BANANA

"Feel too conventional? Wear banana peels as earmuffs!"

POCAAA!

"Want to be happy? Make everyone happy around you!"

The motive of the book

Bello, banana friends! Let me explain our book's super-important mission:

Our "Bananatastic Life Lessons" book isn't just a bunch of silly yellow gibberish - it's a laughter launcher! We've noticed too many humans walking around with faces as droopy as overripe bananas. So, we're on a mission to turn those frowns upside down and make bellies shake like jelly in an earthquake!

But wait, there's more! We're not just after giggles - we want to help people with brain boo-boos too! A big chunk of our banana profits will go to support folks struggling with mental health. The more books we sell, the more help we can give. It's like a banana split where everyone gets a scoop of happiness!

Here's our banana-brilliant idea: Buy a copy to that friend who's always as serious as a banana in a business suit. Maybe even give two - one for each hand! When they read it, they'll go from somber to silly faster than you can say "banana boat"!

Share a photo or video of the book cover on social media with #lifebebanana. Spread the yellow madness! More shares mean more laughs, more books sold, and more support for those who need a mental health boost.

Remember: Life is short like a banana, so make it sweet and a little bit mushy! Buy the book, share the laughs, help others - that's the banana-tastic way to live!

Now go forth and spread the banana joy! Let's make the world a more yellow, giggly place!

And Guess what? We've got a whole bunch of banana-mazing goodies waiting for you in our online store! It's like a banana theme park for your shopping cart! We're talking: and that money will also go to help people with mind-melons. You bought this book and now we know what you will love to buy so Just grab your banana-phone and scan the QR code in the book. It'll take you right to our store faster than you can say "banana split sundae"!

Printed in Great Britain
by Amazon